AN ILLUSTRATED USE
FOR THE APPLE WATCH SE 2020

A How -to- Guide to Getting the Most from Your Apple
Watch SE

Bernard Gates

Table of Contents

Introduction

The Apple Watch SE is one of the current additions to the Apple Watch line up. It was launched on September 18 2020. It's averagely priced and geared towards those who may not have the financial clout to step up to the series 5 and 6 but want something better than the earlier iterations. The Apple watch SE is more than just a watch. It's a combination of health and fitness tracker and motivator, communications connector, emergency contact band and hand wearable computer platform.

The watch SE much like the series 5 runs on the new s5 chip. It is faster than the watch 3 but won't be as fast as the series 6. It has the WatchOS 7 software.

The Watch SE has most of the same features as the watch 3 including fall detection, real-time elevation tracking, optical heart rate sensors, accelerometers, compass, always-on altimeters, microphones and speakers among others but it lacks the ECG app or the blood oxygen monitoring app. Apple has added an international emergency calling function that allows users to have access to assistance by just pushing and holding the side button even without an active cellular plan.

The Watch SE comes with Wi-Fi, GPS, and cellular and it uses the same display as the watch 6. It has a retina LTPO OLED display but doesn't have the always- on feature of the series 5 and 6.

The apple watch is also water resistant to 50 meters.

All Watch SE models are aluminum. Casing colors are silver, gold, space gray and starts from $279 for the 40mm version and $309 for the 44mm version. Let's get started with how to navigate around it.

Chapter 1: Set up and getting started

So, you just purchased your new Apple watch SE and need to get it set up and running. Note the following:

- To setup and start using your Apple Watch, you need an iPhone with the latest version of iOS
- You need to also ensure that you have the Bluetooth of your phone is turned on and there is a Wi-Fi or mobile network connection
  Now take the following steps:
- Turn on the Apple Watch by pressing and holding the side button till you see the Apple logo

- Next, **hold the apple watch close to your iPhone** and wait for the **"Use Your iPhone to Set Up this Apple Watch"** message. If you don't get this message, open the Apple watch app and tap **Start Pairing**

- Keep both devices together until you finish these steps
- Hold the iPhone over the animation by centering the watch face in the **viewfinder** on your iPhone and wait for the successful pairing confirmation message

- If you can't use the camera, you can tap **Pair Apple Watch Manually** at bottom of the screen and follow the steps
- If this is your Apple first watch, tap **Set Up Apple Watch** or alternatively, choose **backup.**
- If asked, update your watch to the latest version of watchOS
- Agree to the terms and conditions and tap **Continue**
- Sign in with your **Apple ID Password** when prompted. If not, you can sign in later from the watch app by tapping General>Apple ID and then sign in
- If Find My is not active on your phone, you will be required to turn on activation lock. If you see an activation lock screen, it means your Apple Watch is linked to an Apple ID. You will need to enter the email address and password for that Apple ID to continue the setup
- Next, choose your settings. Your Apple Watch will show you what settings it shares with your phone.
- Create a passcode by tapping **Create a Passcode** or **Add a Long Passcode.** Switch to the Apple Watch to enter your new passcode. Tap **Don't Add Passcode** if you prefer to do so later. You will also be asked to set up Apple Pay by adding a card

- Next, choose your preferred features and apps. If you have a cellular version of the Apple Watch, you can set up mobile data Wait for your devices to sync. Keep them close until you get a chime and feel a gentle tap from your watch. **Press the Digital Crown**

Pairing Apple Watch SE to Your iPhone

You need to make sure that you have an iPhone 6s or later with iOS 13 or later. The setup assistants on both your phone and watch will work together to help you pair and set up your watch.

- Make sure your iPhone is powered on and close to you
- Put on your watch and make sure it fits well on your wrist
- Press and hold the **side button** to power it on. You should see the Apple logo
- Bring your phone close to the watch and wait for the pairing screen to show on your iPhone and tap **Continue.** You can decide to open the Apple watch app on your iPhone and then tap **Pair New Watch**
- At the prompt, position your phone so that your Apple watch appears in the viewfinder in the Apple watch app. This would pair both devices

- Next, tap Set Up Apple Watch and follow the instructions on both devices to finish the set up

Unpairing an Apple Watch
- Open the Apple watch app on your phone
- Tap **My Watch** and then tap your apple watch at screen top

- Next, tap the ⓘ next to Apple watch you want to unpair and tap **Unpair Apple Watch**

Pairing More than one Apple Watch

It's possible to pair another watch with your iPhone. All you need do is to bring your phone close to the watch, wait for the Apple Watch pairing screen to appear and then tap **Pair** or follow these steps:

- Open the **Apple Watch** app on your iPhone
- Tap **My Watch** and tap your apple Watch at screen top

- Tap **Pair New Watch** and follow the onscreen instructions
  You can set up your watch as new or use a backup of your other watch. Each watch has different settings and you can customize each differently.

Switching to a different Apple Watch

Your iPhone can only detect one watch at a time. To switch to another, you have to put it on and then raise your wrist. If you opt to do it manually, do the following:

- Go to the **Apple Watch app** on your iPhone
- Tap **My Watch** and then tap your Apple Watch at screen top.
- Turn off the **Auto Switch**. The active watch is identified by a white tick inside a yellow circle

To know if your Apple watch is connected to your phone, swipe up from the bottom of your watch screen and open the control center and then look for the green connected status icon.

Pairing Apple Watch SE to a new iPhone
If you are getting a new phone, you need the following:

- Apple ID & Password
- Both old and new phones need to be connected to Wi-Fi
- Your Apple Watch and phone need to be charged at least, 50 percent
- Your Apple watch passcode
  If you have your old iPhone, use these steps to back up your watch before pairing with your new iPhone

- **Update your old phone and Apple watch.** It might take some time so you would want to choose a good time to do so

- **Check your health and activity setting.** If you used iCloud to back up, go to settings> [your name]>iCloud and ensure that health is on. If you used your computer, make sure you encrypt your back up to save your health and activity content

- **Back up your old iPhone via iCloud or your computer. Your** iPhone backs up your computer
- Set up your new iPhone and choose your most recent back up to restore data from your old device to the new one. Make sure that your phone and watch are up to date or you may not view your backup in the list
- Should your phone ask you if you want to use your Apple Watch, tap **Continue.** If you are not asked, you can still do so manually following the steps below:
- Erase your Apple Watch

- Setup your new iPhone 5 and sign in to iCloud. If you have setup and signed in, skip this step
- Open the Apple Watch app on the new device and **Pair your watch** to the new phone
- If your iPhone should ask you to start pairing, **unpair your watch** so you can set it up

  After setup, you can now begin to use your Apple Watch with your new phone

  If you don't have your old iPhone or erased it follow these steps:
- **Erase** your Apple Watch
- Set up the new phone and sign in to iCloud. If you have already done so, you can skip this step
- Open the Apple Watch app on your new device and **pair your watch** to the phone
- Make sure that your phone and watch are up to date and try restoring from a back up
- If you are asked to restore from a watch backup, choose the most recent. If you don't have a backup, you have to set up the Watch as new
- Follow the directions on your screen to finish setting up

  If you have your old iPhone and didn't erase it, do the following:
- **Unpair your watch** from your old iPhone
- If you just restored your new phone from a recent backup, pair both devices. Before doing so, make sure that both devices are up to date
- In case your phone back up is several days or weeks old and you want to preserve as much content as you can, **erase your new iPhone** and then transfer the content from your old iPhone to the new.
- Pair the Apple Watch and your iPhone again

  If the Apple Watch gets stuck while pairing, do the following:
- **Press and hold the digital crown and side button** at the same time until the watch restarts and release the buttons

Digital Crown/
Home button

Side button

- When your watch restarts, press the screen firmly or **press and hold the digital crown**
- Tap **Reset**
- After the watch resets you can proceed to pair with your phone again by bringing the iPhone close to the watch and following the screen instructions
  In case your iPhone fails to ask if you want to use your Apple Watch during setup, here's what to do:
- **Unpair** your watch from your old iPhone
- **Pair** it with the new iPhone
- When prompted, restore your apple watch from a backup. Make sure your watch and phone are up to date.
  If you transferred content to your new phone via your computer but can't find your health and activity content,
- On your old iPhone and new one, **go to settings> [your name]>iCloud and verify that health is turned on**
- **Erase** your new phone and **restore it from new backup**
- **Pair** your Watch and iPhone again. Encrypt your back up if using a computer
  Set up trouble shooting guide
- if your Apple Watch won't turn on, you might need to charge it first
- if you are asked for a passcode, it means your Apple Watch is still paired with another phone. You may need to erase the watch and set it up again if you don't have the passcode

- if you see an activation lock screen, it means that your Apple watch is linked to an Apple ID and you need to enter the email and password for that Apple ID to continue. If the watch was previously owned, you may need to contact the person to remove the lock

  if you can't seem to set up your Apple Watch or get an error message:
- Make sure that your iPhone has the latest iOS
- Turn off and turn your phone
- Turn off and turn on your Apple Watch

Charging the Apple Watch SE

- Make sure you place Apple Watch **Magnetic Cable** or Apple Watch **Magnetic Charging Dock** on a flat surface
- Plug it into the power adapter
- Next plug the adapter into a power outlet

  To begin charging the Apple Watch:
- Place the **charging cable** on the back of the watch. The concave end of the cable should snap to the back of the watch and align properly
- You would hear a chime when the watch starts charging unless it's in silent mode. You would see a green charging symbol that looks like lightning. The symbol would be red if the watch battery is very low and you will see an image of the charging cable
- You can charge the watch in a flat position with its band open or on its side. If you are using the charging dock, lay the watch on it.

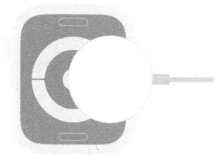

To Check Remaining Power

- **Swipe up** from the watch screen bottom to open control center. You can add a battery complication to the watch face to check the remaining power easily

View the percentage of remaining battery life.

To Save Power When the Battery is Running Low

- **Swipe up** from bottom of the watch screen to open **control center**
- Tap the **battery percentage** and then drag the **power reserve slider** to the right

When battery power drops to 10 percent or lower, you Apple Watch will alert you and give you the option of activating the power reserve mode

Returning to Normal Power Mode

Restart your Apple watch by pressing and holding the side button until the Apple Logo appears. The battery must have at least 10 percent charge to restart

Checking the Time Since the Last Charge

- Open the **watch app** on your iPhone
- Tap **My Watch** and then go to **General** and view **Usage**

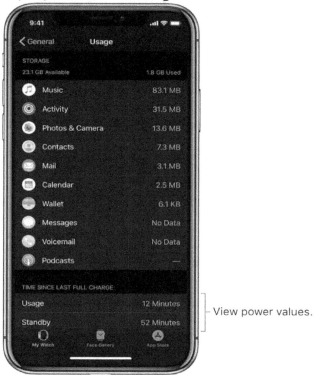

View power values.

Chapter 2: Basics
Telling Time and Settings
Raise your wrist: the time appears on the watch face in the clock in grid view and at top right of most apps

Hear the Time:

- Go to **Settings** on your watch. **Tap Clock.** Turn on **speak time. Hold two fingers** on watch face to hear the time
- Your watch can also play chimes on the hour. From the **Settings** app, tap **Clock** and turn on **Chimes**. Tap **sounds** to select your preferred one.
- You could ask Siri: raise your wrist and say "what time is it?"

Feeling the Time (Taptic Time)
Your watch can tap out the time on your wrist with a series of distinct taps
- Open **Settings** on your watch
- Tap **clock**, navigate up and tap **Taptic Time**
- Turn on **Taptic Time** and select a setting between **Digits, Terse** or **Morse** code
- To set up Taptic Time on your Phone, open the **Apple Watch** app, tap **My Watch**, go to **Clock> Taptic Time** and turn it on

Waking the Apple Watch Display
- You can raise your wrist. The watch goes back to sleep when you lower your wrist
- You can wake the watch by tapping the display or by pressing the digital crown
- You can wake the watch by turning the Digital Crown upward. To do this, you would have adjusted the setting by going to **General>Wake screen**, then **Turn on Wake Screen on Crown Up**

Setting Your Watch to Wake to Your last activity
- Open **Settings** on your watch
- Go to **General**>Wake screen and ensure that Wake Screen on Wrist Raise is turned on

- Navigate down and select when you want your Apple Watch to wake to your last used app. Choose from Always, Within 1 hour of Last Use, Within 2 Minutes of Last Use, or Never Unless in Session

Keeping the Apple Watch Display on Longer
- From the **Settings** app on your Apple Watch
- Go to **General**> **Wake Screen** then tap **Wake for 70 Seconds**

Locking or Unlocking the Apple Watch
You have the option of unlocking the watch via a passcode or you can set it to unlock automatically when you unlock your iPhone

- For passcode, key in the **passcode** and then tap **OK**
- For the second option, open the Apple Watch app on your iPhone, tap **Passcode** and then turn on **Unlock With iPhone.** Your iPhone has to be within normal Bluetooth range of your watch to unlock it. If your watch Bluetooth is off, use the passcode to unlock it

Changing Your Passcode
- From the **Settings** app on your watch
- Tap **Passcode**, tap **Change Passcode** and then follow the screen instructions
- You can equally open the Apple Watch app on your phone, tap **My Watch**, tap **Passcode,** tap **Change Passcode** and follow the directions

Turning off the Passcode
- Open the **Settings** app on your App
- Tap **Passcode** and tap **Turn Passcode Off**

- You can also open the Apple Watch on your phone, tap **My Watch,** tap **Passcode** and tap **Turn Passcode off**

Locking the Apple Watch Automatically
- Open **settings** on your watch
- Tap **Passcode** and **Turn on Wrist Detection**

Locking your Watch Manually
- **Touch and hold**, then **swipe up** from bottom of watch screen to open **control center**
- Tap the padlock symbol

- To lock manually, you must turn off wrist detection by opening the **Settings** app on your watch, tap **Passcode** and then **turn off wrist detection**

Erase Apple Watch After 10 Unlock Attempts
If you lose your watch or if its stolen, you can set it to erase after 10 attempts to unlock it using a wrong password

- Open **Settings** on your Watch
- Tap **Passcode** and turn on **Erase Data**

Changing the Language and Orientation on Your Apple Watch
- Open the Apple Watch app on your iPhone
- Tap **My Watch,** go to **General>Language & Region,** tap **Custom,** then tap **Watch Language**

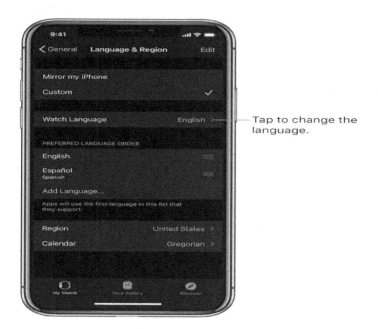

Tap to change the language.

Switching Wrists or Digital Crown Orientation

- Open the **Settings** app on your Apple Watch
- Go to **General> Orientation**

Alternatively, you can access the Apple Watch app on your iPhone, tap **My Watch**, go to **General> Watch Orientation**

Using the Compass on Apple Watch

You can view your bearing at top left. Turn the **Digital Crown** to navigate up and see your incline, elevation and coordinates

- Launch the **Compass** app on your watch
- For more precise bearings, hold the watch flat to align the crosshairs at compass center

- To add a bearing, turn the **Digital Crown** to navigate up, tap **Add bearing,** turn the watch to the bearing and tap **Done**
- To edit the bearing, turn the **Digital Crown** to navigate up, tap **Edit Bearing,** turn the watch to new Bearing and tap **Done**
- To clear the bearing, turn the **Digital Crown** to navigate up and tap **Clear Bearing**

Crosshairs aligned

Turning on Airplane Mode

Touch and hold screen bottom and swipe up to launch Control Center and tap

Turn airplane mode on or off.

Ask Siri. Say something like "Turn on airplane mode"

To put both your iPhone and watch in airplane mode using one step:

- Open **Apple Watch** on your phone. Tap **My Watch.** Go to **General> Airplane Mode.** Turn on **Mirror iPhone.**

- When both devices are within Bluetooth range of each other, anytime you switch to airplane mode on one device, the other replicates

Turning on the Apple Watch Flashlight

Turn on: Touch and hold screen bottom, swipe up to launch control

center. Tap ⬜ and **swipe left** to select a mode between steady white light, flashing white light or steady red light

Turn off: press the **Digital Crown** or **side** button or **swipe down** from top of watch face.

Using Theater Mode on Apple Watch

Touch and hold screen bottom, swipe up to open Control Center,

tap ⬜ and tap theater mode

Turn theater mode on or off.

- To wake Apple Watch when in Theater mode, tap the **display,** press the **Digital Crown** or **side** button or turn the **Digital Crown**

Turning on Silent Mode

- Touch and hold the bottom of the screen, swipe up to open

Control Center and tap 🔔

- You can also from your phone, launch the **Apple Watch** app, tap **My Watch**, tap **Sounds and Haptics** and turn on silent mode

Turning on Do Not Disturb

- Touch and hold the screen bottom, swipe up to launch Control Center, tap 🌙 and choose an option: On, On for 1 hour, On until this evening, On until I leave and On till end of event

- You can also launch the **Settings** app on your watch, tap **Do Not Disturb** and turn on **Do Not Disturb**

   To turn it on automatically when you begin a workout:

- From the **Settings** app on your watch, tap **Do Not Disturb** and turn on **Workout Do Not Disturb**
- You can do it from your phone by launching the **Watch** app, go to **General**> **Do Not Disturb** and then turn on **Workout Do not Disturb**

Turning Sleep Mode on or Off

- Tap and hold the screen bottom and swipe up to launch **Control Center,** tap ⛉. You can leave sleep mode for a short while by turning the Digital Crown to unlock

Locating Your iPhone with your Watch

- Touch and hold screen bottom and swipe up to launch Control Center 📳
- Your phone makes a tone so you can find it
- In the dark, touch and hold the Ping iPhone button and iPhone will flash
- If your iPhone isn't in range of your watch, you can use Find My from iCloud.com

Finding your Apple Watch with Find My

If you misplace your watch, you can use Find My locate it

- Launch the **Find My** app on your phone
- Tap **Devices** and tap your watch from the list
- You can play a sound on your watch, tap **Directions** to see directions to it in **Maps**, mark it as lost or erase it

Choosing an Audio Output
- **Touch and hold** screen bottom and **swipe up** to launch **Control Center**
- Tap  and choose the device you want to use

Handing off Tasks from Apple Watch
This feature lets you move from one device to the other without interrupting what you are doing.

- Unlock your iPhone
- If you have an iPhone with Face ID, **swipe up** from bottom edge and pause to show the **App Switcher.** If you have an iPhone with a Home button, double click the Home button to show the **App Switcher**
- Tap the button that shows at screen bottom to open same item on your iPhone

Using your watch to unlock your Mac
You have to have a mid-2013 or later mac with macOS 10.13 or later.

- From your Mac, select **Apple menu> System Preferences**
- Click **Security & Privacy** and click **General**
- Select "**Use Your Apple Watch to Unlock apps and your Mac**
  If you have more than one watch, you need to specify which one you want to use. Your mac must have Wi-Fi and Bluetooth turned on

- Unlocking your mac is as simple as waking it up. No password needed as long as you are wearing your watch and you're your Mac

Adjusting Brightness, Text size, Sounds and Haptics on Apple Watch
Adjusting brightness and text:

- Launch **Settings** on your watch. Tap **Display and Brightness** to adjust the following:

  Brightness: Tap the **brightness controls** to adjust, or tap the **slider** and turn the **Digital Crown**

  Text Size: tap **Text Size**, tap the letters or turn the **Digital Crown**
  Bold Text: Turn on **Bold Text**
- To do this from your Phone, open the **Watch** app, Tap **My Watch**, tap **Display and Brightness** and then adjust brightness and text

  Adjusting Sound:
- Launch **Settings** on your watch. Tap **Sounds & Haptics**
- Tap the **volume controls** under **Alert Volume** or tap the **slider** then turn the **Digital Slider** to Adjust

- To do it via your Phone, open the **Apple Watch** app, tap **Sound and Haptics** and drag the **Alert Volume** slider

- To reduce loud sounds coming from headphones connected to your watch, from **Sounds & Haptics** in Apple Watch, tap **Reduce Loud Sounds** and turn on **Reduce Loud Sounds**

Adjusting Haptic Intensity:
- Launch **Settings** on your Apple Watch
- Tap **Sounds & Haptics.** Turn on **Haptic Alerts**
- Choose between **Default** or **Prominent**

- To do it from your phone, open the **Apple Watch** app, tap **My Watch,** tap **Sounds & Haptics,** choose between **Default or Prominent**

Turning Digital Crown Haptics off or on:
- Launch the **Settings** app on your Apple Watch
- Tap **Sounds & Haptics.** Turn **Crown Haptics** off or on
- To do it from your phone, open the **watch app,** tap **My Watch,** tap **Sounds & Haptics**. Turn **Crown Haptics** off or on

- Next, tap **My Watch** to view the settings for your Apple Watch

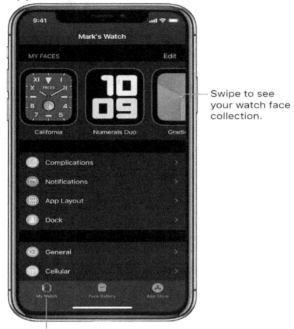

Swipe to see your watch face collection.

Settings for Apple Watch.

Removing, Changing and Fastening Apple Watch Bands

Before you change your Apple Watch band, ensure the following:

Make sure that you are replacing a band with one of the same size

Ensure that you use a band that matches your Apple Watch case size. It's possible for you to use a band designed for any of the Apple Watch series line up as long as the sizes can match. As a guide, bands for 38mm and 40mm cases work with each other and bands for 42mm and 44mm cases also work with each other

Removing and Changing Bands

- Press the **band release button** on your Apple Watch
- Next, **slide the band** across to remove it and then slide the new band into position

If you encounter trouble removing or inserting a band, press the band release button again. Do not attempt to force a band to fit in the slot

Fastening a Band

- Make sure that the watch fits closely on your wrist for optimal performance
- For best results, the back of the Apple Watch needs skin contact for functions like wrist detection, haptic notifications etc to work.
- Wear the watch with the right fit—not too tight and not too loose –so the sensors can work optimally. The sensors only work when you wear the watch on top of your wrist

Chapter 3: Setting up Handwashing on Apple Watch SE

- Open the **Settings** app on your watch
- Tap **Handwashing**
- Turn on **Handwashing Timer**
- When your watch detects that you have started washing your hands, it would start a 20 second timer. To know when you have washed enough, you can turn on Haptics in the Handwashing screen

Receiving Handwashing Notifications

You can set up your watch to a get reminder to wash your hands when you get home. You must set up a home address in your My Card in the Contacts app on your phone to get handwashing reminders

- Open the **Apple Watch** app on your phone
- Tap **My Watch**. Tap **Handwashing**. Turn on **Handwashing Reminders**

Viewing a Report of Your Average Handwashing Times

- Open the **Health** app on your phone
- Go to **Browse>Other Data.** Tap **Handwashing**

Chapter 4: Using Cycle Tracking on Apple Watch

Women can use the app to log and monitor details of their menstrual cycle. Using the information, the app can alert the user when it predicts that the next period or fertile window is about to begin. You need iOS 14 for this feature.

- Open the **Health** app on your phone
- Tap **Browse** at lower right to view the Health Categories screen
- Tap **Cycle Tracking**
- Tap **Get Started** and follow the directions to set notifications and other options
- Navigate to bottom. Tap **Options** and turn on the options you want

Logging Your Cycle on Apple Watch

- Open the Cycle Tracking app on your watch
- Tap the buttons to choose options that describe your period
- The details you provide will show up in the Cycle Log on iPhone. If you activated **Period Prediction** and **Fertility Prediction** in the Health app on your phone, you will receive notifications on Apple Watch about upcoming periods and fertility windows

Chapter 5: Staying Connected with Apple Watch SE

When you are not with your phone, you can still stay in touch with family, friends and colleagues.

Sending a Message with Siri

- Say something like, 'Tell Esther I would be back in 30 minutes'
- Lower your wrist to send

Creating a message on Apple watch

- Go to **Messages** on your watch
- From the screen top, tap **New Message**
- Tap **Add Contact,** tap a contact from the list of recent conversations that shows and then choose an option: you could search for someone in your contacts or dictate a number, choose from your list of contacts or tap the number pad to enter a phone number

Replying to a Message

- Turn the **Digital Crown** to navigate to the bottom of the message
- Choose how to reply

Dictate your response.

Scroll to see more smart replies.

Send a digital touch.

Responding Quickly with a Tap Back

- **Double tap** a specific message in a conversation
- Tap a **Tapback**

Double-tap a message, then tap to choose a Tapback.

Replying to One Message in a Conversation

- From a **Messages** conversation
- Touch and hold a **specific message** to reply to
- Tap **Reply**
- Create your response and then tap **Send**

Composing a message on Apple Watch

There are several ways to compose a message on your Apple Watch

- **Send a smart reply**: scroll to view a list of handy phrases you can use. You just tap to send
  To add your own phrase:
- Open the Watch app on your phone
- Tap **My Watch,** go to **Messages**> Default Replies, tap **Add Reply**
- To customize the default replies, tap **Edit** and drag to reorder them or tap the red delete button to delete one

Turn to see more replies.

Tap a message to send it.

You can send a message by dictating text:

- Tap the **microphone** icon
- Say what you want to
- Tap **Done**
  You can also speak punctuation as you dictate.
  You can create an audio clip:
- Open the **Apple Watch** app on your phone
- Tap **My Watch**
- Go to **Messages>Dictated Messages**
- Tap Transcript, Audio, or Transcript or Audio. If you tap audio, the recipient gets your dictated text as an audio clip not as a text to read. If you tap transcript or audio, you can choose the message format.

You can scribble a message:

- Tap  then write your message
- Turn the **Digital Crown** as you write to predictive text options
- Tap one to select it
- Tap **Send**
- Tap at lower left to choose a different language

Turn to see predictive text options, then tap one to choose it.

Write your message.

Sending Emoji

- Tap
- Tap a category
- Scroll to browse available images
- Tap on the Selected one to send

Sending a Memoji Sticker

- Tap
- Tap an image in the Memoji Stickers collection
- Tap on a variation to send it

Sending a Sticker

- Tap
- Navigate to bottom and tap More Stickers
- Tap on one to send

Chapter 6:Using Apple Pay to send and Receive Money

Using Siri: say something like, 'Send Esther $100" if you have more than one Esther in your contacts, you would be asked to specify which one

- Open the **Messages** app on your Apple Watch
- Start a new conversation or continue an existing one
- Tap
- Turn the **Digital Crown** or tap the + or – button to select a whole dollar amount

  To send an amount not in whole dollars, for e.g $15.25, tap the dollar amount, tap after the decimal and turn the Digital Crown to choose a value
- Tap **Pay,** confirm the payment and double click the side button to send

When payment is complete, you will get a confirmation message.

The payment is made from your Apple Cash Balance but if it's not enough, the balance is paid with a debit card

Canceling a Payment
If the receipt hasn't been accepted, you can cancel a payment

- Open the **Wallet** app on your watch
- Select a **card** and scroll to see the transactions list
- Tap on the unpaid transaction and tap **Cancel Payment**
  To do it from your phone:
- Open the **Apple Watch** app on your phone
- Tap **My Watch, Tap Wallet** and **Apple Pay**, tap **Apple Cash** card, tap **Transactions**, tap the **unpaid transaction** and tap **Cancel Payment.**

Requesting a Payment from Apple Watch
You can use Siri to request a payment. Say something like: "Ask Esther to send me $200"

Sending a message:

- Open **Messages** on your watch
- Start a new conversation or selecting an existing one and tap

- Swipe left on the **Pay** button, enter an amount and tap **Request** When you use Apple Payment for the first time, you have to agree to the terms and conditions on your phone before accepting the payment. Subsequent payments are accepted automatically unless you opt to accept the payments manually

Responding to a Payment Request on Apple Watch
- Tap the **Pay** button that appears in the payment request in Messages
- Turn the **Digital crown** or tap buttons on the screen to change the amount if desired
- Tap **Pay** and double click the side button to make the payment

Viewing Transactions Detail on Apple Watch
Viewing transactions via Messages:

- Open the Messages app and tap an Apple Pay message to view a transaction summary
  Viewing transactions in Wallet:
- Open the **wallet** app on your Apple Watch**,** tap a **Card,** scroll to view transactions **and** tap a **transaction** for details
  To view all Apple Cash transactions on your iPhone
- **Open the Wallet app on your Phone:**
- Tap **My Watch,** tap **Wallet & Apple Pay**
- Tap your **Apple Cash Card**, tap **Transactions**
  Receive a PDF statement of your Apple Cash Transactions by Email:
- Tap your **Apple Cash card.** Tap **Transactions. Swipe** to bottom and tap **request Transaction Statement**

Chapter 7: Using Apple Watch SE with a Cellular Network

You can use a cellular connection on your watch to make calls, reply to messages, receive notifications and do more. Ensure the following:

- Your phone and watch must have the latest software
- Check for updates to your carrier settings
- You must have an eligible cellular service plan with a supported carrier. Your phone and watch must use the same carrier and you must be within your carrier's network when you set up cellular on your watch

Setting Up Your Cellular Plan:

> If you have a cellular capable watch, you can activate your cellular plan when you first set up your watch. During set-up, look for the cellular option and follow the on-screen steps. If you didn't set up cellular when you first set up your apple watch, you can do it by following the steps below

- Launch the **Apple Watch** app on your phone
- Tap the **My Watch** tab. Tap **Cellular**.
- Tap **Set Up Cellular**
- Follow the instructions for your carrier

Changing Carriers

- Open the **Apple Watch** on your iPhone
- Tap the **My Watch** tab. Tap **Cellular**.
- Your watch will switch automatically to the carrier your phone uses. If you want to add a new plan, **tap Add a New Plan** and follow the steps

Transferring Your Cellular Plan to a New Apple Watch

- Deactivate the cellular plan from your old watch
- Pair the new watch with your phone. During set up, **tap Set Up Cellular**
- Some carriers will allow you to transfer your existing plan to your new watch directly from the **Apple Watch** app

- In case you don't see an option to move your cellular plan, contact your carrier

Removing Your Cellular Plan:
- Open the **Apple Watch** app on your iPhone
- Tap the **My Watch tab.** Tap **Cellular**
- Tap the **information button**  next to your cellular plan at screen top
- Tap **Remove Carrier Plan.** Repeat tap to confirm

Setting up Cellular on a Family Member's Apple Watch

You can set up a cellular Apple Watch for a family member who do not own an iPhone. If your cellular carrier supports the use of a managed Apple Watch, you have the option to add the watch to your plan during setup. If your carrier doesn't support it, you can use an alternative carrier.

To see the phone number assigned to your family member's Apple Watch after you set up cellular, go to **Settings** on the watch, then tap **Phone.**

Using Dual SIM with Apple Watch GPS + Cellular models

If you set up multiple cellular plans using Dual SIM on your compatible iPhone, you can use both plans on your Apple Watch. You only have to choose which one your watch uses when it connects to cellular networks.

Setting up Multiple Cellular Plans

If you set up Dual SIM on your iPhone XS, iPhone XS Max, or iPhone XR or later, you can add both cellular plans on your Apple Watch Series 5 as long as each plan is eligible and from a supported carrier.

You can set up one plan when you set up your watch initially. Then you can set up your second plan later in the Apple Watch app:

- From your iPhone, open the **Apple Watch** app.

- Tap the **My Watch** tab. Tap **Cellular.**

- Tap **Set Up Cellular** or **Add a New Plan**. If you didn't add your first plan during setup, you can add it here.

- Follow the onscreen guide to choose the plans that you want to use on your Apple Watch.

Switch Between Plans

- From your iPhone, open the **Apple Watch** app.

- Tap the **My Watch** tab. Tap **Cellular.**

- Your plan should automatically switch. If this doesn't happen, tap the plan that you want to use.

  - You can also switch plans directly from your Apple Watch. Go to **Settings** > **Cellular or Settings** > **Mobile Data,** then choose the plan that you want your watch to use when it connects to cellular.

How Your Apple Watch Receives Calls and Messages

When your Apple Watch is Paired with your iPhone, you can get calls and messages from both plans. Your watch displays which cellular plan you received a notification from by showing a badge with the first letter of the line. If you respond to a call or message, your watch will respond from the line that you received the call or message from.

When your Apple Watch is not close to your iPhone and connected to cellular, you can still get calls and messages from your active plan. If your iPhone is turned on, even if it isn't nearby, you can get messages and notifications about calls from your other plan. If you respond to a call, your watch automatically calls back from your active plan. If you respond to an SMS message, your watch automatically texts back from the plan that you received the message on. You can respond to iMessages as long as there's an active data connection from any plan. If you wish to change your active plan, you can manually switch between plans from Settings on your Apple Watch.

Making Calls on Apple Watch
Using Siri: Tell Siri Something like: "Call Esther" or "Dial 555 555 1234"

Or Call Esther on Facetime audio"

Making a call:

- Open the **phone** app on your Apple Watch
- Tap **Contacts** and turn the **Digital Crown** to scroll
- Tap the **Contact** you want to call and tap the phone button
- Tap the **FaceTime Audio** to start a FaceTime audio call or tap a **phone number**
- Use the **Digital Crown** to adjust volume during the call

Entering a phone number on Apple Watch:
- Open the **phone** app on your watch

- Tap **Keypad,** key in the number and tap
- In a call, you can use the **keypad** to enter additional digits. Tap

  and tap **the keypad** button

Chapter 8:Making calls Over Wi-Fi

You can use your Apple Watch to make and receive calls over a Wi-Fi network even if your iPhone is not with you or turned off. Your Apple Watch just has to be within range of a Wi-Fi your phone has connected to previously. You also need to make sure your carrier supports Wi-Fi calling.

- From your iPhone, go to **Settings>phone**, tap **Wi-Fi calling**, turn on both **Wi-Fi Calling on This iPhone** and **Add Wi-Fi Calling for Other Devices**
- Open the **Phone** app on your Apple Watch

- **Choose a contact and tap**
- Choose the **phone number** or **FaceTime** address you want to call
  You can view call information on your Apple Watch in the **Phone** app when you are making a call on your iPhone. You can also end the call with your watch.

Connecting Apple Watch to a Wi-Fi

- To select a Wi-Fi network, open the **Settings** app on your watch
- Tap **Wi-Fi** and tap the name of an available network
- If you have to enter a password, you have 3 options:
  - ✓ Use your finger to scribble the password character on the screen.
  - ✓ Tap and enter the password on another device
  - ✓ Choose a password from the list
- Tap **Join**

Forget a Wi-Fi Network

- Launch **Settings** on your watch. Tap **Wi-Fi** and tap the network name. Tap **Forget This Network**

Connecting Apple Watch to Bluetooth Headphones or Speakers

You can play audio from your watch via Bluetooth headphones or speakers even without your phone nearby

- Launch **Settings** on your watch. Tap **Bluetooth**
- Tap the device when it appears

Disconnecting from Wi-Fi

- You can disconnect your watch from a Wi-Fi connection and switch to a cellular connection if your watch has a cellular function
- **Touch and hold** the bottom of the screen, swipe up to launch **Control Center** and tap  in **Control Center**

Tap to disconnect from Wi-Fi.

Chapter 9:Using Apple Watch SE to get Directions or Contact a Friend

- Open the **Find People** app  on your watch
- Tap **your friend,** scroll down, tap **Directions** to open the **Maps** app
- Tap the **Route** to get step by step directions from your current location to your friend's location

Using Find People to Contact a Friend

- Open the **Find People** app on your watch
- Tap **your Friend.** Scroll down and tap **Contact** to call, email or use Walkie-talkie or send a message to your friend

Using Find People to Announce Your Arrival

Open the **Find People** app. Tap **Your Friend.** Tap **Notify [your friend's name],** and choose to notify your friend when you arrive at their location

Chapter 10: Using the Walkie Talkie Feature of the Apple Watch SE

This requires that both participants have a Bluetooth to iPhone connection, Wi-Fi or cellular. It works like a regular walkie-talkie.

Inviting a Friend to Use Walkie-Talkie

- Open the **Walkie-Talkie** app  on your watch for the first time
- Scroll down your contacts list and tap a **name** to send an invite

- If your contact accepts the invite, you both can start a conversation when you are available
- To add another contact, tap **Add Friends** on the Walkie-Talkie screen and choose a contact

How to have a Walkie-Talkie Conversation

- Open the **Walkie-Talkie** app on your watch
- Tap **your friend's name**
- Touch and hold the **Talk** button to speak
- If your friend is available, walkie-talkie opens on their watch and they will hear what you said
- Use the **Digital Crown** to adjust the volume while talking

Talk with a Single Tap:

You can use a single tap to talk if you have difficulty in keeping your hand on the talk button

- Open the **Settings** app on your watch
- Tap **accessibility** and below Walkie-Talkie, turn on **Tap to Talk**
- When this is on, tap once to talk and tap again when you are done talking
  To do this from your Phone:
- Open the **Apple Watch** app on your phone
- Tap **My Watch.** Tap **Accessibility.** Below Walkie-Talkie, turn on **Tap to Talk**

Removing a Walkie-Talkie Contact

- From the **Walkie-Talkie** app on your watch, **swipe left** on a contact and tap X

Make Yourself Unavailable in Walkie Talkie

- Touch and hold the screen bottom and swipe up to view control center

- Scroll up and tap
- Alternatively, in the Walkie-Talkie in your Apple Watch, scroll to screen top and turn off Walkie-Talkie

Chapter 11: using Apple Watch Apps
Opening Apps on Apple Watch

From the home screen, you can access any app on your watch. You can also use the Dock to get quick access the apps you use the most. You can add up to 10.

Displaying Your Apps on a Grid or in a List

- Open the **Settings** app on your watch
- Tap **App View**. Tap **Grid View** or **List View**
- From your phone, you can open the **Apple Watch** app, tap **My Watch**, tap **App view** and tap **Grid View** or **List View**

Opening Apps from the Home Screen

Grid view: Tap the app icon. If you are looking at the Home screen, you can turn the Digital Crown to open the app in the center of the display

From the watch face, press to see the Home Screen.

Tap to open an app.

List view: Turn the **Digital Crown** and then tap an app

Turn the Digital Crown to browse the apps.

Tap to open an app.

Returning to the Home Screen from an App

- Press the **Digital Crown** once and then press again to switch back to the watch face

- To view the last opened app while on another, double click the **Digital Crown**

Opening an App from the Dock

- Press the **side** button, turn the **Digital Crown** to scroll through the apps in the Dock
- Tap an app to open

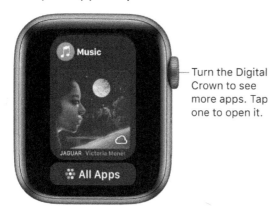

Choosing which Apps that Appear in the Dock
From recently used apps:

- Open the **Apple Watch** app on your phone. Tap **My Watch**. Tap **Dock**. Tap **Recents**
- The most recently used app appears at the top of the dock with others below in the exact order they were last accessed

From favorite apps:
- Open the **Apple watch** app on your phone. Tap **My Watch**. Tap

  Dock. Select **favorites**. Tap **Edit** and tap ⊕ next to the apps you want to add.

- Drag ≡ to adjust their order
- When you select favorites, the most recently used app appears at the top of the dock allowing you to open it. To add it to the dock, tap **Keep in Dock**

Removing an App from the Dock

- Press the **side** button. Turn the **Digital Crown** to app you want to remove.
- Swipe left on the app and tap X

Swipe left on an app, then tap the X.

- To switch back to the Home screen from the dock, navigate down to dock bottom and tap **All Apps**

Organizing Apps on Apple Watch

Rearrange your apps in grid view:

- From your watch, press the **Digital Crown** to return to Home Screen
- If the screen is in list view, open the **Settings** app on your **Apple Watch**, tap **App View** then tap **Grid View**
- Press the **Digital Crown, touch and hold an app** till they all **jiggle** and drag it to a new position

Touch and hold an app, then drag to a new location.

- Press the Digital Crown when you are done
- Alternatively, from your phone, open the **Watch** app, tap **My Watch**, Tap **App View** and Tap **Arrangement. Touch and hold an app icon** to drag to a new location

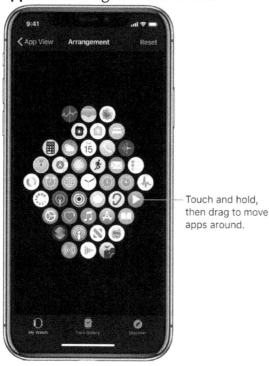

Touch and hold, then drag to move apps around.

Removing an App from Apple Watch
Grid view:

- From the **home screen, touch and hold the app** icon till you see an **X** on it.
- Tap the **X** to remove from your watch. It will still be in your phone unless you delete it there too

List view: swipe the app to the left and then tap the dustbin icon to delete it from your watch. Unless you do the same for your phone, it will remain there

Adjusting App Settings
- Open the **Apple watch** app on your phone
- Tap **My Watch** and navigate down to view installed apps
- Tap an app to change its settings
  Some restrictions you set on your phone may affect the watch also. For e.g, if you deactivate camera on your phone, the camera icon is also removed from your watch home screen

Getting More Apps

- Open the **App Store** app  on your watch
- Turn the **Digital Crown** to browse featured apps
- Tap a **category** or tap **See All** below a Collection to view more apps
- To get a free app, tap **Get**. To buy an, tap the **price**
- To find a specific app, tap the **search field** at screen top and use dictation or scribble to enter the name of the app.
- If you are using a cellular enabled watch, cellular data charges may apply

Installing Apps you have on iPhone
- Open the **Apple Watch** app on your phone
- Tap **My Watch.** Tap **General** and turn off **Automatic App Install**
- Tap **My Watch** and scroll down to view **Available Apps**
- Tap **Install** next to the apps you want to install

Chapter 12:Using Control Center on Apple Watch SE

From control center, you can check the battery, silence your watch, turn on Do Not Disturb and much more

Opening or Closing Control Center:

swipe up from Watch Face. From other screens, **touch and hold** screen bottom and **swipe up**

Closing Control Center:

 Swipe down from screen top or press Digital Crown
You can't open control center from the home screen on your watch. You have to press the digital crown to go to the watch face or from an app, open the control center

Apple Watch   Apple Watch with Cellular

Touch and hold the bottom, then swipe up to open Control Center.

Rearranging the Control Center

- **Touch and hold** screen bottom and **swipe up** to open the control center
- Navigate to bottom of **Control Center** and tap **Edit**
- **Drag** a button to new Position and tap **Done**

Removing Control Center Buttons

- **Touch and hold** screen bottom and swipe up to launch the **Control Center**
- Navigate down to screen bottom and tap **Edit**
- Tap ⊖ in the corner of the button you want to remove and tap **Done**

Restoring a Control Center Button

- Open **Control Center**. Tap **Edit** and tap in the corner of the button you want to restore and tap **Done**

Chapter 13: Using Siri on Apple Watch SE

Siri is the intelligent personal assistant that helps you get things done

Setting up siri:

- From your paired iPhone, tap **Settings> Siri & Search.**
- Ensure that **Listen for "Hey Siri"** is on. On iPhone X or later, confirm that **Press Side Button for Siri** is on. On iPhone 8 or earlier, confirm that **Press Home for Siri** is on
- From your watch, tap **Settings> Siri**
- Choose if you want to turn **Hey Siri** and **Raise to Speak** on or off
- Confirm that your watch or phone can connect to the internet

Raise your wrist:

- Raise your wrist to wake your watch
- Hold the watch close to your mouth
- Say what you want

Turning the Raise to Speak Feature off or on:

- Go to **Settings** on your watch. Tap **Siri.** Turn **Raise to Speak on** or off

Press the Digital Crown:

- Hold down the **Digital Crown**
- When the listening indicator shows, say what you need

- Release the **Digital Crown**

Say "Hey Siri":

- **Raise your wrist** or tap the **screen** of your watch
- When it wakes, say "Hey Siri" and say what you need

Changing Voice Feedback Settings:

- Open the **Settings** app on your watch
- Tap **Siri** and then select from the following:
  Always On
  Control with Silent Mode
  Headphones Only

Chapter 14: Seeing and Responding to Notifications

your watch can show notifications as they arrive such as messages, noise alerts, invitations, reminders etc. Unread notifications are shown by a red dot at the top of your watch face

Responding to a notification:
- When a notification arrives, **raise your wrist** to see it
- Turn the **Digital Crown** to navigate to notification bottom and tap a button there
- You can equally tap the app icon in the notification to open the corresponding app

Clearing a Notification:
- **Swipe down** on it or navigate to the bottom and tap **Dismiss**
- To clear a notification without reading it**, swipe to the left** and then tap **X**
- To clear all notifications, scroll to screen bottom and tap **Clear All**

Viewing Notifications you haven't Responded to:
- From the watch face**, swipe down** to open Notification Center

- From other screens, **touch and hold the screen top** and then **swipe down**
- **Swipe up or down** or turn the **Digital Crown** to scroll the notifications list
- Tap the **notification** to read and respond to it

Choosing how notifications are delivered
- Open the **watch app** on your phone. Tap **My Watch.** Tap **Notifications**
- Tap the app [Messages], tap **Custom.** Select an option from:
  Allow Notifications
  Send to Notification Center
  Notifications Off

Choose which notifications to see on Apple Watch.

- You can manage notifications preferences from your watch by swiping left on a notification and tapping ● ● ● . Options include:
  Deliver Quietly
  Turn off on Apple Watch

How to silence all Notifications on Apple Watch

- Touch and hold screen bottom, swipe up to open the Control Center

- Tap 🔔

- You will still feel a tap when you get a notification but to stop

  sounds and taps, touch and hold screen bottom and tap 🌙

Chapter 15:Using Shortcuts on Apple Watch SE

With short cuts, you can get things done with just one tap.

Run a Shortcut:

- Open the **Shortcuts** app on your watch and tap a shortcut

Adding a Shortcut Complication

- Touch and hold the watch face and tap **Edit**
- Swipe left to the **Complications** screen and tap a **Complication**
- Navigate to **Shortcuts** and choose a shortcut

Adding More Shortcuts to Apple Watch

- Launch the Shortcuts app on your phone

- Tap at top right corner of a shortcut

- Tap on the shortcut screen and turn on **Show on Apple Watch**

Chapter 16: creating an Emergency Medical ID

- Open the **Health** app on your phone.
- Tap your profile picture at the top right and tap **Medical ID**
- Tap **Get started** and enter your information

Viewing your Medical ID on Apple Watch

- On your watch, hold the side button until the slider shows
- Drag the Medical ID slider to the right

In case you don't see your medical ID when you hold the side button on your Apple Watch:

- Open the **Apple Watch** app on your iPhone. Tap **My Watch**. Tap **Health**. Tap **Medical ID**. Tap **Edit**. Turn on **Show When Locked.**

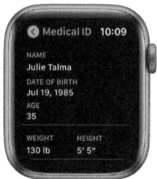

Setting up Fall Detection on Apple Watch

The fall detection feature connects you to emergency services and messages your emergency contacts. If you fall and remain immobile for a minute, your watch will make a call to emergency services automatically

- Open the **Settings** app on your watch
- Go to **SOS>Fall Detection**. Turn on **Fall Detection**
- You can do it from your phone: open the **Apple Watch** app on your phone. Tap **My Watch**. Tap **Emergency SOS** and turn on **Fall Detection**
  If you turn off wrist detection, you watch won't make the call even after it has detected a fall

Chapter 17: setting up a Family member's watch

You can set up and manage Apple Watch for a family member without access to their own iPhone. To do so, you have to be the family organizer or parent/guardian in your family sharing group. The watch must be a cellular enabled Watch SE, a series 4 or later. The cellular carrier must not be the same as the iPhone its paired to.

Setting the Watch Up:

- **Erase** the watch to make sure there's no content in it
- Let the family member put on the watch and make sure it fits comfortably on the wrist
- Turn on the watch by pushing and holding the **side** button till the Apple logo appears
- Bring your iPhone near the watch. Wait for the Apple Watch pairing screen to appear on your phone. Tap **Continue**
- You can also open the Apple Watch app from your phone. Tap **All Watches**. Tap **Pair new Watch**
- Tap set up for a family member. Tap **Continue** on the next screen
- At the prompt, place the phone so that the watch appears in the view finder in the watch app
- Tap **Set Up Apple Watch**. Follow instructions on the phone and watch to finish the set up

Managing a Family Member's Watch

- Launch the **Apple Watch** app on the phone used to manage the watch
- Tap **All Watches**. Tap a watch under **Family Watches**. Tap **Done.**
- When you tap My Watch for a managed watch, you will view a group of settings.
- Adjust or change any setting you want to

Setting Up Screen Time

You can use screen time to configure controls for a family member's watch. You can also set limits on iTunes store and app purchases, explicit content and location information

- Launch the **watch app** on the control iPhone used to manage the watch
- Tap All Watches. Tap the watch under **Family Watches**
- Tap **Done.** Tap **Screen Time.** Tap **Edit Screen Time Settings**
- Tap settings such as **Downtime** and **Content & Privacy Restrictions** to edit them

- You can also launch the **Settings** app on your iPhone. Tap **Screen Time.** Tap your **family member's name** under the **family heading** and select a **setting**

Setting Up Reminders on a Family Member's Watch

It's important to upgrade your iCloud reminders on a managed Apple Watch to have the advantage of additional Siri interactions, create all day reminders and join lists shared by others.

Upgrading Reminders
- Launch the **Settings** app on the managed Apple Watch
- Tap **reminders.** Tap **Upgrade**

Setting a Notification for All-Day Reminders
- Launch **Settings** on the managed Apple Watch
- Tap **Reminders.** Turn on **Today Notification** to show the time. Tap the time
- Next, enter the time you want notifications to appear. Tap **Set**

Choosing a Default List
Reminders created outside a given list appear in the default setting

- Launch **Settings** on the managed watch
- Tap **Reminders.** Tap the **current list setting**
- Tap the **list** you want to be the default

Setting Up School Time on Apple Watch
This feature limits Apple Watch features during school hours, allowing a family member to focus on learning and participation.

- Launch the **watch app** on the control iPhone
- Tap **All Watches.** Tap the **watch** under **Family Watches**
- Tap **Done.** Tap **Schooltime**
- Turn on **Schooltime.** Tap **Edit Schedule**
- Select **days and times** you want **Schooltime** to be active
- Tap **Add Time** if you want to set up multiple schedules during a day

- To change the Schooltime schedule at a later time, open the **Apple Watch** app on the phone, tap 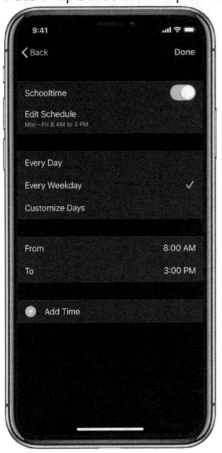 next to the managed watch. Tap **Schooltime**. Tap **Edit Schedule**

Exiting Schooltime

The schooltime setting can be temporarily exited when its active if the wearer wants to check other settings or functions

- Tap the display. Turn the **Digital Crown**. Tap **Exit**

If the schooltime setting is exited during scheduled hours, the setting returns when the wrist is lowered. During nonscheduled hours, schooltime remains inactive until the next scheduled time or you tap

 in the Control Center

See When Schooltime Was Unlocked

- Launch the **watch app** on the control iPhone
- Tap **All Watches**. Tap the Watch under **Family Watches**
- Tap **Done**. Tap **Schooltime**
- Swipe up to view reports for the days, times and duration Schooltime was unlocked. To view the report on the watch, go to **Settings** and tap **Schooltime**.

Viewing Activity and Health Reports for Family Members

If you set up daily activity goals for your family member, you can see how active that family member is each day and their health information with the person's authorization.

Viewing an Activity Report

- When you set up activity goals for your family member, launch the **Health app** on your phone
- Tap B**rowse.** Tap the family member name under **Shared Health Data**. Tap **Activity**.
- Tap the timeline to see how active the family member was up to the time of day

Viewing Health Information
- Open the **Health app** on your phone. Tap **Browse**
- Tap the family member's name under **Shared Health Data**
- Tap **Health Categories** and tap a **category**

Adding Health Details and Medical ID
- Launch the Apple Watch app on the control iPhone used to manage the watch
- Tap **All Watches**. Tap the watch under **Family Watches**
- Tap **Done**. Tap **Health** and choose from one of the following:
  1. Tap **Health Details** to enter or edit information such as birthdate, height and weight
  2. Tap **Medical ID** to add emergency contacts and more

You can use the control iPhone to view the health and medical data of the family person.

- On your iPhone: launch the **Health app**. Tap **Browse**. Tap the person's name. Tap **Profile**
- On the managed Watch: launch **Settings** and tap **Health**

Chapter 18: Apple Watch Faces

Users of the Apple Watch can change and customize the watch face, choose complications and add watch face collections to their gallery. All of this can be done from the face gallery in the Apple Watch app.

Opening the Face Gallery

- Open the Apple Watch app on your iPhone
- Tap Face Gallery

Tap a face to customize it and add it to your collection.

Choosing Features for a Face

- From the **Face Gallery**, tap a face. Tap a **feature** a such as color or style
- Play around with different options. The face at the top changes as you do so and it would enable you make sure the design is to your taste

Adding Complications in the Face Gallery

- From the **face gallery**, tap a face. Tap a complication position which could be **Top Left, Top Right** or **Bottom**
- Swipe to view the available complications for the position and tap the one you want.
- If you don't want a complication in that position, navigate to top of the list and tap **Off**

Adding a Face
- After customizing a face in the **Face Gallery**, tap **Add**
- To switch to the new face on your Apple Watch, swipe left till you see it

Customizing the Watch Face
Choosing a different watch face:

- **Swipe** the watch from **edge to edge** to view the faces in your collection
- To view all watch faces, touch and hold the **watch face**, swipe to your preferred one and tap it

Swipe left or right to see other watch faces.

Add features to your watch face.

Adding Complications to the Watch Face:
Complications are special features that you can add to some watch faces so you can check or view things like stock prices, weather report etc or information from other installed apps
- Make sure that the **watch face** is showing, touch and hold the display and tap **Edit**
- **Swipe left** all the way to the end. If a face offers complications, they would be displayed on the last screen
- Tap a **Complication** to choose it. Turn the **Digital Crown** to select a new one
- Press the **Digital Crown** when done and tap the face to switch to it

Turn to scroll through options.

Adding Complications from Other Apps
- Go to the **Apple Watch** app on your iPhone
- Tap **My Watch**. Tap **Complications**

Adding a Watch Face to Your Collection
- With the current face showing, touch and hold the display
- **Swipe left** all the way to end. Tap the **New** button (+)
- Turn the **Digital Crown** to browse watch Faces. Tap the one you want to add
- You can customize after adding

Tap new, scroll to browse watch faces, then tap a face to add it.

Viewing Your Collection
- Open the **Apple Watch** app on the iPhone
- Tap **My Watch**. Swipe through your collection below **My Faces**

Deleting a Face from Your Collection
- Touch and hold the display with the current watch face showing
- Swipe to the unwanted face. Swipe it up and tap **Remove**
- From your iPhone, go to the **Apple Watch** app, tap **My Watch**, tap **Edit** in the **My Faces area. Tap** ⊖ next to the watch face you want to delete. **Tap Remove**

Swipe up to delete a watch face, then tap Remove.

Setting the Watch Ahead
- Launch the Settings app on your watch
- Tap Clock.
- Tap +0 min, turn the digital Crown to set the watch ahead with as much as 59 mins

Sharing Apple Watch Faces
You need watchOS 7 to be able to this. The recipient watch must also be watchOS 7 enabled

- On **Apple Watch,** show the watch face you intend to share

- Touch and hold the display and then tap ⬆️
- Tap **Add Contact** to add a recipient. Tap **Create Message** to compose your message
- Tap the watch face name then tap **"Don't include"** for any complications you don't feel like sharing
- Tap S**end**
- In the alternative, you can launch the **Apple Watch** app, tap a **watch face** from your face gallery or collection. Tap ⬆️ then select a sharing option

Receiving a Watch Face

watch faces can be received via messages or mail or clicking a link online

- Open a text, email or link that contains a shared watch face
- Tap the **shared watch face** and tap **Add**
- If you get a watch face with a complication from a third-party app, you can tap the **app price** or download it from the app store. if you are not interested, you can tap **Continue Without This App** to get the watch face without the complication

Apple watch Faces and their Features
Activity Analog

- This watch face shows your activity progress superimposed over a normal analog clock

Activity Digital

- This is the opposite of the analog activity face. It shows the time in a digital format in addition to your activity progress

Artist

This face changes anytime your wrist or tap the display

Astronomy

This face displays a continuously updating 3D model of the moon, Earth or solar system

Turn to move forward or back in time.

Breathe

This watch face enables you to relax and breathe mindfully

California

This watch face has a mix of Roman and Arabic numerals. Its available on watch SE, Apple watch series 4 and later

Chronograph

This watch face measures time in accurate increments. It also has a stopwatch that can be activated right from the watch face

Chronograph Pro

This watch face is only for the watch SE, Apple Series 4 and later. If you tap the bezel surrounding the main 12-hour dial on the watch face, it turns into a chronograph.

Color

This watch face can show the time and any feature of your choice in any color of your choosing.

Count up

This watch face is for tracking elapsed time and is only available on the Watch SE, series 4 and later

Explorer

This watch face displays 4 prominent green dots in the center that denote cellular signal strength. Its only available on Apple watches with cellular

Fire and Water

This watch face animates when you raise your wrist or tap the display

GMT Face

For watch SE, series 4 and later, it features two dials: a 12-hour inner dial that displays local time and a 24-hour outer dial that allows you monitor a second time zone

Gradient face

This features gradients that moves with the time. For Watch SE, series 4 and later.

Info graph Face

This watch has up to 8 complications and sub dials. For watch SE, series 4 and later

Info graph Modular face

This is another variation of the info graph face. Available on Watch SE, series 4 and later

Kaleidoscope Face

This face enables you choose a photo to create a watch face with changing patterns of shapes and colors

Liquid Metal Face

This watch face animates whenever you raise your wrist or tap the display

Memoji Face

This watch face shows all the Memoji you have created and all Memoji characters.

Meridian Face

This face has a classic look with 4 sub dials

Mickey and Minne Mouse

This face uses the popular cartoon characters to display the time using their hands to show the hours while their feet tap out the seconds

Modular Face

This watch face has a digital time display and grid layout that makes it possible for you to add features to give you a view of your day

Modular Compact Face

This watch face allows you choose up to 3 complications as well as a digital or analog dial

Motion Face

This watch face shows a beautiful animated theme

Numerals Face

This watch face shows the time using analog hands. Users can select from 7 different typefaces and lots of colors for a good combination

Numerals Duo

This face uses large font made for Apple Watch to display large number

Numerals Mono

This face shows large numbers in font designed by Apple for Apple Watch

Photos Face

This watch face makes it possible for you to use a photo or more from the photo app on your watch to customize the screen display.

Pride Analog Face

This face was inspired by the rainbow flag. The colors move when you tap the face or turn the Digital Crown

Pride Digital

Simple

This watch face allows you to add detail to the dial and features to the corners

Siri Face

This face allows siri take a look at day and displays useful information. Use the Digital Crown to scroll through your day

Solar Face

This face shows the sun's position in the sky and day, date and time. This based on your location

Turn the Digital Crown to move through the day's solar events.

Solar Dial Face

This face shows a 24-hour circular dial that monitors the sun as well as an analog or digital that moves opposite to the sun's trajectory

Stripes Face

This watch face lets you choose the number of stripes you want, colors and rotate the angle

Time-lapse Face

This face displays a time lapse video of a natural setting or cityscape of your choosing

Toy story Face

This watch face brings your favorite toy story characters to life with a raise of the wrist

Typograph Face

This watch face uses 3 custom fonts

Utility Face

This is a practical and functional watch face that lets you add up to 3 complications

Vapor Face

This watch face animates whenever you raise your wrist or tap the display

x-Large Face

This watch face is useful when you need the largest available display. A complication fills the screen when you add it

Chapter 19: Adding an Alarm on Apple Watch SE

- To use Siri, say something like: "set repeating alarm for 4 a.m."

- To do it manually, go to the **Alarms** app  on your watch
- Tap **Add Alarm**. Tap **AM** or **PM**. Tap the hours or minutes
- Turn the **Digital Crown** to Adjust then tap **Set**
- To turn the alarm on or off, tap its switch. You can also tap the alarm time to set repeat, label and snooze options

Turning off the snooze feature

- Open the **Alarms** app on your watch
- Tap the **alarm** in the **alarms list** and turn off snooze

Deleting an Alarm

- Open the **Alarms** app on your watch
- Tap the **alarm** in the list
- Navigate to bottom and **Delete**

Skipping a Wake-up Alarm
- Open the **Alarms** app on your watch
- Tap the alarm that shows under **Sleep| Wake Up** and tap **Skip for Tonight**

Viewing the Same Alarms on iPhone and Watch
- Set up the alarm on your phone
- Launch the **Apple Watch** app on your phone
- Tap **My Watch.** Tap **Clock.** Turn on **Push Alerts from iPhone**

Setting Up Apple Watch as a Nightstand Clock with Alarm
- Launch the **Settings** app on your phone
- Go to **General> Nightstand Mode.** Turn on **Nightstand Mode**

When the alarm sounds, press the **side button** to deactivate it or press the **Digital Crown** to snooze it for 9 minutes

Press to snooze.

Press to turn off alarm.

Chapter 20: Adding Audiobooks to Apple Watch SE

- Go to the **Apple Watch** app on your Phone
- Tap **My Watch.** Tap **Audiobooks**
- Tap **Add Audiobook** and select audiobooks to add to your watch

Playing Audiobooks on Apple Watch

- Connect your watch to Bluetooth headphones or speakers and

  open the **Audiobook**s app  on your watch
- Turn the **Digital Crown** to navigate through the artwork
- Tap on an Audiobook to play it

Playing Audiobooks from Your Library

If your watch is close to your iPhone, or connected to a Wi-Fi or cellular network, you can stream audiobooks from your library to your watch.

- Got to the **Audiobooks** app on your watch
- Tap **Library.** Tap on an **audiobook** to play it
- To play audiobooks bought by members of your family sharing group, tap **My Family** on the audiobook screen and tap an audiobook.

Using Siri to play an Audiobook

- Ask Siri to play an audiobook. You can say "play the audiobook Treason"

Chapter 21: Using Apple Watch to Breathe Mindfully

- To start a breathe session, launch the **Breathe app**  on your watch
- Tap **Start**. Inhale slowly as the animation expands and exhale as it shrinks

Setting the Duration of a Breathe Session
- Launch the **Breathe** app on your watch
- Turn the **Digital Crown** to increase the duration. Choose one and five minutes
- To use this as your default duration, open settings on your watch, tap **Breathe**, turn on **Use Previous Duration**

Viewing your Heart Rate During Breathe Sessions
- Launch the **Health app** on your phone
- Tap **Browse**. Tap **Heart**. Tap **Heart Rate**
- Tap **Show More Heart Rate** Data. Swipe up and tap **Breathe**

Chapter22: Using Calendar on Apple Watch SE
Viewing calendar events on Apple Watch:

- Ask Siri: say something like: "what's my next event?"

- To do it manually, launch the **Calendar app** 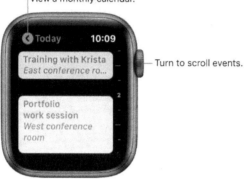 on your watch or tap **the date** or **calendar event** on watch face

- Turn the **Digital Crown** to scroll through scheduled events

View a monthly calendar.

Turn to scroll events.

Adding, Deleting or Changing an Event

- To use Siri, say something like "create a calendar event titled facetime with Dad for December 25 at 10 a.m."
- To delete an event, tap an event, tap **Delete**, tap **Delete Event**
- To change an event, do it with the calendar app on your phone

Adjusting Calendar Settings

- Launch the **watch app** on your phone
- Tap **My Watch**. Tap **Calendar**
- Tap Custom under **Notifications** or **Calendars**

Chapter 23: Using Camera Remote and Timer on Apple Watch SE

Choose options.

Take a photo.

You can use your watch as a remote-control device for your iPhone to take photos, view camera image, set a timer and do more. To do this, your watch has to be within normal Bluetooth range of your phone.

To Take a Photo:

- To use Siri, say: "take a Picture"

- Launch the **Camera Remote** app on your watch
- Place your phone in such a way that you can frame the shot using your watch as a view finder
- Use the **Digital Crown** to zoom
- Tap the key area of the shot in the preview on your phone to adjust exposure
- Tap the **shutter button** to take the shot

Using Your Watch to Review Your Photo Shots

Use the following actions to review your shots on your Watch.

- To View a photo: Tap the thumbnail at bottom left.

- To See other photos: Swipe left or right.

- To Zoom: Turn the Digital Crown.

- To Pan: Drag on a zoomed photo.

- To Fill the screen: Double-tap the photo.

- To Show or hide the Close button and the shot count: Tap the screen.

- When you're finished, tap **Close.**

Choosing a Different Camera and Adjust Settings

- Open the **Camera Remote** app on your Watch.

- Tap , then choose from among the options

Chapter 24: Controlling your Home with Apple Watch SE

You can use the home app to control and automate home kit enables accessories like lights, locks and more. All from your wrist.

When you open the Home app initially on your phone, the set-up assistant would enable you create a home. Accessories and scenes you add on your phone are accessible via your watch too.

- Ask Siri: say something like: "Turn off the kitchen lights"

Adding a new Accessory or Scene to the App

- Go to the **home app** on your phone to set an item as a favorite and tap Rooms
- **Swipe left or right** to locate the accessory or scene and touch and hold it
- Tap Settings then turn on **Include in Favorites**
- When you add a new accessory or scene to your favorites, it would appear in the Home app on your Apple Watch

Controlling Smart Home Accessories and Scenes

- From your watch, open the **home app**

- Tap  for an accessory. Adjust your settings
- **Swipe left** to see more options
- To return to the accessories list, tap **Done**

- To control a scene, open the **Home app** on your watch. Tap a **scene** to turn on or off

Chapter 25: Reading Mail on Apple Watch SE

- To read a message, raise your wrist when you get the notification
- To dismiss the notification, swipe down from the top or tap **Dismiss** at end of the message
- If you didn't see the notification when it came, **swipe down** on the watch face later to view unread notifications
- To control email notifications on your watch, open the Apple **Watch app** on your phone, tap **My Watch,** go to **Mail>Custom**

Read Mail in the Mail App

- Open the **Mail app** on your watch
- Turn the **Digital Crown** to navigate the message list
- Tap on a **message** to view it

Chapter 26: Adding Music to Apple Watch SE

Adding Albums and Playlists to Apple Watch:

- Launch the Apple Watch app from your phone
- Tap **My Watch.** Tap **Music**
- Below **Playlists & Album,** tap **Add Music**
- Choose albums and playlists to add to your watch

Removing Music from Apple Watch

- From your phone, open the **watch app**
- Tap **My Watch.** Tap **Music**
- Turn off any automatically added playlists you don't want on your watch
- To remove other music, you added to Apple Watch, tap **Edit,** tap ⊖ next to the unwanted item

Playing Music on Apple Watch

Use the music app 🎵 to select and play music on Apple Watch

- To use Siri, say something like "play "I know" by Luther Vandross"
- To play music, turn the **Digital Crown** to scroll through album artwork and tap a **playlist** to play
- To play music downloaded to your Apple Watch, tap **Downloaded** and choose music
- To Listen to Apple Music, raise your wrist, request an artist, Album, song, genre or portion of a song lyric

Tap for more options.

Play Music for You

If you're an Apple Music subscriber, you can play music chosen just for you.

- Open the **Music app** on your Apple Watch.

- Scroll to the top of the screen, then tap **Listen Now** to see a curated feed of playlists and albums according to your preference

- Tap a **category**, tap an **album** or **playlist**, then tap ▶ .

- If you tap a station, it plays in the Radio app on Apple Watch

Tell Music What you like, Add Music to the Library, and More

On Apple Watch you can add music to your library, remove songs, mark what you do and don't like, add songs to the queue, browse an artist's music, and view the contents of albums and playlists. Do any of the following:

- View options from the Now Playing screen: While playing music, tap •••, then choose an option.

- View options in Listen Now and Library: **Swipe left** on a song, playlist, or album; tap •••; then choose an option.
  Tap ＋ to add the item to your library.

Using Apple Watch to Control Music on a Mac or PC

Use the **Remote app** on your Apple Watch to play music on a computer that's on the same Wi-Fi network.

Adding and Removing a Music Library

- Open the **Remote** app on your Apple Watch.

- Tap **Add Device.**

  - If you're using the Music app on a Mac with macOS 10.15 or later: Open Apple Music and choose your device from the list of devices shown with your library.

  - If you're using iTunes on your Mac or PC: Click the **Remote button** near the top left of the iTunes window.

- Enter the **4-digit code** displayed on your Apple Watch.

- To control **playback** from your watch, use the **play back controls** in the **remote app.** Use the **Digital Crown** to adjust the volume

- To remove a media Library, launch the **Remote app** on your watch, touch and hold a device

- When the device icon jiggles, tap X to remove it. Tap **Remove**

Recording and Playing Voice Memo on Apple Watch

- Open the voice memo app  on your watch

- Tap ● to begin the recording

- Tap ■ when you are done

- To play a memo, open the **Voice Memo app** on your watch, tap a **recording** on the voice memo screen and tap ▶ to play it

- To delete the recording, tap ••• and tap **Delete**

Chapter 27: Measuring Noise Levels with Apple Watch SE

This feature measures the sound level in your vicinity. When the level gets too much, the watch notifies you.

Setting Up the Noise App

- Open the **Noise app** on your watch
- Tap **Enable** to turn on monitoring
- To measure the environmental noise in your vicinity at a later time, open the **Noise app** or use the **Noise complication**

Getting Noise Notifications

- Go to **Settings** on your watch
- Go to **Noise> Notifications** and select a setting

Reducing Loud Sounds

Your Apple Watch can limit the loudness of your headphone audio to a set decibel level

- Launch **Settings** on your watch
- Tap **Sounds & Haptics.** Tap **Reduce Loud Sounds**
- Turn on **Reduce Loud Sounds** and set a level

Turn off Noise Measuring

- Launch **Settings** on your watch
- Go to **Noise>Environmental Sound Measurements**
- Turn off **Measure Sounds**

Chapter 28: Managing the Photo Album on Apple Watch SE

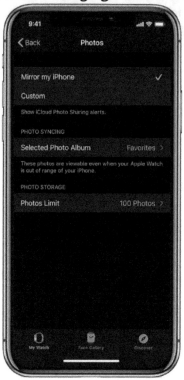

Choosing an album on Apple Watch:

- Open the **Apple Watch** app on your phone
- Tap **My Watch**. Go to **Photos> selected Photo Album** and select the album
- To remove a Photo from Apple Watch, open the **Photos app** on your phone and remove the image from the **synced album**

Taking a screen shot of Apple Watch

- Open the **Settings** app on your watch
- Go to **General** and turn on **Enable Screen shots**
- Push the **Digital Crown** to take a picture of the Screen

Viewing Photos on Apple Watch

Tap to view a photo.

- On Apple Watch, view your photos in the **Photos app**  and show a photo on your watch face.

Browsing photos on Apple Watch

Open the **Photos app** on your Apple Watch and use these actions to search your photos.

- Tap a **photo** to view it.

- **Swipe left or right** to browse other photos.

- Turn the **Digital Crown** to zoom, or drag to pan a photo.

- Zoom all the way out to view the **entire photo album.**

Swipe left or right to
see the next photo.

Turn to zoom.

Drag to pan.

Double-tap to fill
screen or see all.

Chapter 29: Adding Podcast to Apple Watch SE

- Open the **watch app** on your Phone
- Tap **My Watch.** Tap **Podcasts**
- Tap **Custom** and turn on the stations and shows you want to sync to your watch

Playing Podcasts on Apple Watch

- Open the Podcasts app  on your apple Watch
- Turn the Digital Crown to navigate through the artwork
- Tap on a podcast to play it
- You can also ask Siri to play a Podcast

Chapter 30: Controlling Apple TV with Apple Watch SE

Your watch can be used as a remote control for an Apple TV as long as both devices are on the same network

Pair your Apple Watch with Apple TV

If your iPhone has never been on the Wi-Fi network that the Apple TV is on, join it and follow these steps:

- Open the **Remote app** on your Apple Watch.

- Tap your **Apple TV**. If you don't see it listed, tap **Add Device.**

- On the Apple TV, go to **Settings > Remotes and Devices > Remote App and Devices,** then select Apple Watch.

- Key in the **passcode** shown on your Apple Watch.

When the pairing icon shows next to Apple Watch, you can use it to control the Apple TV.

Use your Apple Watch to control Apple TV

Ensure the Apple TV is awake and follow these steps:

- Open the **Remote app** on your Apple Watch.

- Select your Apple TV, then swipe up, down, left, or right to navigate through the Apple TV menu options.

- Tap to choose the selected item.

- Tap the Play/Pause button to pause or resume playback.

- Tap the Menu button to go back, or touch and hold it to return to the main menu.

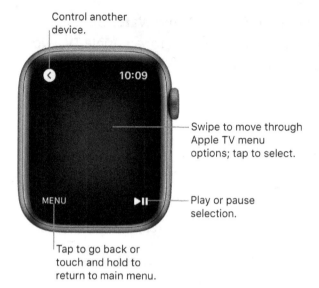

Control another device.

10:09

Swipe to move through Apple TV menu options; tap to select.

MENU ▶️❚❚

Play or pause selection.

Tap to go back or touch and hold to return to main menu.

Unpair and remove Apple TV

- On the Apple TV, go to **Settings > Remotes and Devices > Remote App and Devices.**

- Tap your Apple Watch under **Remote App,** and tap **Unpair Device.**

- Open the **Remote app** ▶️ on your Apple Watch and, when the "lost connection" message shows, tap **Remove.**

Chapter31: Tracking your sleep with Apple Watch SE

- To set up sleep, open the **Sleep app** on your watch
- Adhere to the onscreen instructions

Change or Turn off your Next Wake-up Alarm

- Go to the **Sleep app** on your watch
- Tap your current bed time
- To set a new wakeup time, tap the wakeup time, turn the **Digital Crown** to set a new time. Tap **Set**
- If you don't want your watch to wake you in the morning, turn off the alarm

Viewing your Recent Sleep History
- Open the Sleep app on your watch
- Navigate down to see the amount of sleep you got the previous night and your average sleep over the past 14 days

Chapter32: Viewing Stock Data in Apple Watch SE

- Launch the **Stocks app** on your watch
- Tap a **stock** in the list
- Tap < at top left corner to return to the stocks list or use the **Digital Crown** to move to the next stock in the list

Adding and removing a stock:

- To add a stock, go to screen bottom, tap **Add Stock.** Scribble or say the name of the stock and tap **Done.** Tap **stock name** in the list
- Removing a stock is as easy as swiping left on the stock you want to remove and tap X

Choosing the Stock Data you View

- Open the **Settings** app on your watch
- Go to **Stocks>Data Metric, tap Current Price, Points Change, Percentage change or Market Cap**

Displaying stock information on Watch Face

- First off, add the stock complication to the watch face
- Open the **watch app** on your phone
- Tap **My Watch,** tap **Stocks** and select a default stock

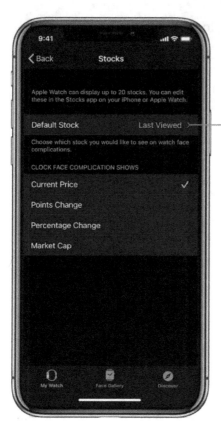

Choose the stock shown on your watch face.

Chapter33: Working out with Apple Watch SE
Staying Fit with Apple Watch

You can keep tabs on your keeping fit activity with your watch and have a more active life. Your watch will assist with reminders and friendly competitions

Close Each Ring

The Apple Watch tracks how much you move, stand and exercise each day.

- You can set goals using the **activity** app and check your progress throughout the day
- Navigate down for more details such as total steps and distance
- Your watch will let you know when you complete a goal

To use Siri, say something like "start a 500-calorie bike ride"

Starting a Workout

- Open the **Workout** app
- Tap type of **workout**
- Check your progress on the screen
  In case you forget to start a workout before exercising your watch will prompt you to open the workout app and credit you for the exercise you have done.

Cycling

The Apple Watch makes It easier to workout using a bicycle providing you with directions, maps, and show bike lanes and busy roads. You need WatchOS 7 for this feature.

Comparing Current Activity Statistics with Past Ones

You can check how well you are progressing compared to a previous year. You can do this via the trends feature

- Open the **Fitness** app on your iPhone
- Tap the **Summary** tab
- Swipe up to view your **activity metrics**

Tracking Important Health Information
It's possible for you to use the Apple Watch for health stuff like setting sleep goals, track important heart data, keep tabs on your oxygen blood levels and reminders to wash your hands

Setting Sleeping Timetable
- Go to the **Health** app on iPhone
- Create a **sleep schedule**
- Wear your watch to bed and Apple Watch takes it from there

Getting Heart Health Notifications
- Open the **Apple Watch** app on your phone
- Go to **My Watch**
- Tap **Heart**
- Turn on **High Heart Rate** or **Low Heart Rate**
- Set a Heart Rate Threshold
- Turn on **Irregular Rhythm** notifications

Starting a Workout

- launch the **Workout app** 🏃 on your Apple Watch.

- Turn the **Digital Crown** to the workout you are interested in.

- Tap **Add Workout** at screen bottom for sessions like Tai Chi or kickboxing.

- Tap ••• to set a goal

- Choose a calorie, time, distance, or open goal (an open goal setting means that you've set no particular goal but still want your Apple Watch to track your workout).

- Turn the **Digital Crown** or tap + / – to set.

- When you're ready to go, tap **Start.**

Tap to set workout goals.

Turn the Digital Crown to choose another workout.

Combining Multiple Activities in a Single Workout

- Launch the **Workout app** on your Apple Watch.

- Start your first workout—an outdoor run, for example.

- When you're ready to begin a different activity—like an outdoor bike ride—swipe right, tap , then select the workout.

- When you finish all your activities, swipe right and tap **End.**

- Turn the **Digital Crown** to scroll through the results summary.

- Scroll to the bottom and tap **Done** to save the workout.

Setting a target pace for an Outdoor Run Workout

Enter a target pace for an outdoor run, and your Apple Watch will tap you on the wrist to advice you know if you're ahead or behind a set pace after one mile.

- Launch the **Workout app** on your Apple Watch.

- Turn the **Digital Crown** to navigate to Outdoor Run, then

  tap   .

- Tap **Set Alert**, then tap **OK.**

- Adjust the **target time** for running a mile—9 minutes, for example—and tap **Done.**

- Choose **Average or Rolling**, then tap <.

Average is your average pace for all the miles you've run. Rolling is your one-mile pace taken at that moment.

Using Apple Watch During a Workout

Your Apple Watch can be an active partner even during your workout. While working out you can do the following:

- Check your progress: Raise your wrist to see your workout stats, including your goal completion ring, elapsed time, average pace, distance covered, calories consumed etc.

- Pausing and resuming the workout: To pause the workout when you wish, press the **side button** and the **Digital Crown** at the same time. For all workouts except swimming workouts you can also swipe right on the workout screen and tap Pause. To continue, tap Resume.

- Mark a segment of your workout: Double-tap the display to indicate a segment of your workout. You briefly get to view the stats for that segment. To see all your segment stats after the workout, open the **Fitness app** on your iPhone, tap **Workouts**, tap the workout, then navigate down.

- Music while you work out: During a workout, swipe left to the Now Playing screen to choose music and control the volume on your Bluetooth headphones. To choose a playlist that plays automatically when you begin a workout, open the **Apple Watch app** on your iPhone, then tap **My Watch**. Tap **Workout**, tap **Workout Playlist**, then choose a playlist.

Ending and Reviewing Your Workout on Apple Watch

- When you reach your goal, you will get a tone and feel a vibration. If you want to continue, your Apple Watch continues to collect data until you stop it. When you're ready:

- Swipe right, then tap **End.**

- Turn the **Digital Crown** to navigate through the results summary, then tap **Done** at the bottom

- To review your workout history, launch the **Fitness app** on your phone. Tap **Summary**. Tap a **workout**

Starting a Swimming Workout
- Launch the **workout app** on your watch
- Select **Open Water Swim** or **Pool Swim**
- To pause or resume while swimming, push the **side button** and **Digital Crown** simultaneously
- To view your swimming summary, unlock your Watch and tap **End**

Manually Clear Water after Swimming

- Touch and hold the bottom of the screen, swipe up to open

  Control Center, then tap

- Turn the **Digital Crown** to unlock the screen and clear water from the speaker.

Pairing your Apple Watch with Gym Equipment

- Check if the equipment is compatible. You will get a "Connects to Apple Watch" or "Connect to Apple Watch" message on the equipment.

- Ensure that your watch is set to detect gym equipment. To do this, open the **Settings app**  on your Apple Watch, tap **Workout**, then turn on **Detect Gym Equipment**.

- Hold your Apple Watch within a few centimeters of the contactless reader on the gym equipment, with the display facing the reader.

- A gentle tap and beep will let you know that your Apple Watch is paired.

Starting and Ending a Workout

- Press **Start** on the gym equipment to begin. Press **Stop** on the equipment to end the workout.
- When you end your workout, data from the equipment appears in the workout summary in the Activity app on your Apple Watch and the Fitness app on iPhone.

Updating your height and weight

- Launch the **Apple Watch app** on your iPhone.

- Tap **My Watch, go to Health > Health Details,** then **tap Edit.**

- Tap **Height or Weight,** and make changes

Changing Your Workout View

- Launch the **Apple Watch app** on your iPhone.

- Tap **My Watch,** go to **Work out > Workout View,** then tap **Multiple Metric** or **Single Metric.**

- To choose which stats are shown for each workout type—for example, if you want to see your current elevation while you're hiking in the mountains—tap the **workout type,** tap **Edit,** then add or delete stats and drag to reorder.

- During your workout, turn the **Digital Crown** to highlight a different metric—distance or your heart rate, for example.

Changing Measurement Units

If you prefer meters to yards or kilojoules to calories, you can change the measurement units the Workout app uses.

- Launch the **Settings app** on your Apple Watch.

- Tap **Workout,** scroll to the bottom, then tap **Units of Measure.**

- You can change units for energy, pool length, cycling workouts, and walking and running workouts.

Pause running workouts automatically

- Launch the **Settings app** on your Apple Watch.

- Tap **Workout,** then turn on **Running Auto Pause.**

- Your Apple Watch automatically pauses and resumes your outdoor running workout—for example, if you stop to cross the street or get a drink of water.

Turning Workout Reminders on or off

- Launch the **Settings app** on your Apple Watch.

- Tap **Workout,** then change the **Start Workout Reminder and End Workout Reminder** settings. (Workout reminders are on by default.)

- You can also open the **Apple Watch app** on your iPhone, tap **My Watch,** tap **Workout,** then change the workout reminder settings.

Avoiding accidental taps

If the exercise you are doing or the gear you are wearing causes accidental taps on your Apple Watch, you can lock the screen so an accidental tap does not happen.

- Lock the screen: Swipe right, then tap **Lock.**

- Dismiss a notification: Press the **Digital Crown.**

- Unlock the screen: Turn the **Digital Crown**.

Conserving Power During a Workout

You can extend battery life on Apple Watch during walking and running workouts.

- Open the **Settings app** on your Apple Watch.

- Tap **Workout,** then turn on Power Saving Mode

Chapter 34: Using World Clock on Apple Watch SE

Use the **World Clock app**  on your Apple Watch to check the time in cities around the globe.

Ask Siri. Say something like: "What time is it in London?"
Adding and Removing Cities in World Clock

- Launch the **World Clock app** on your Apple Watch.

- Tap **Add City.**

- Tap the Dictation, Scribble, or Keyboard button, then enter the city name.

- Tap the **city name** to add it to World Clock.

- To remove a city, **swipe left** on its **name** in the **city list**, then tap **X.**

Checking the Time in Another city

- Launch the **World Clock app** on your Apple Watch.

- Turn the **Digital Crown** or swipe the screen to scroll the list.

- To see more information about a city, including time of sunrise and sunset, tap the **city** in the list.

- When you are finished, tap < in the top-left corner, or **swipe right** to return to the city list.

World Clock   10:09
Cupertino
10:09AM
Today

— Turn to scroll through cities.

New York
1:09PM
Today, +3HRS

Sydney

Using the stop Watch

- Open the **Stop watch app**  on your watch or tap the stop watch on your watch face

Starting, Stopping and Resetting the Stopwatch

- Open the **Stopwatch app** on your Apple Watch, and do any of the following:

- Start: Tap the green Start button.

- Record a lap: Tap the white Lap button.

- Record the final time: Tap the red Stop button.

- Reset the stopwatch: Tap the white Reset button or the Lap button.

- The timing continues even if you switch back to the watch face or open other apps.

Start or stop the stopwatch.

Record lap times.

Changing the Stopwatch Format
- Launch the **Stopwatch app** on your watch
- Tap the display to select from **Digital, Analog, Graph** and **Hybrid** formats

Setting a Timer on Apple Watch
- To use Siri, say: "set a timer for 1 hour"
- In the alternative, launch the **Timer app** on your watch
- Tap a **timer duration** to begin the timer
- Navigate down to select a recent or custom time

- To create a custom timer, launch the timer app on your watch
- Scroll down and tap **Custom**
- Tap hours, minutes or seconds and turn the **Digital Crown** to adjust
- Tap **Start**

Tap hours, minutes, or seconds, then turn the Digital Crown.

Chapter 35: restarting, resetting, restoring and updating Apple Watch SE

If your watch SE starts malfunctioning or something isn't working right, you can try restarting your Apple Watch and its paired iPhone.

Restarting Apple Watch SE

- Turn off your Apple Watch: Press and hold the **side button** until the sliders appear, then drag the **Power Off slider** to the right.

- Turn on your Apple Watch: Hold down the **side button** until the Apple logo appears.

You can't restart your Apple Watch while it's charging.

Restart the paired iPhone

- Turn off your iPhone: For versions with **Face ID,** press and hold the **side button** and a **volume button**, then drag the slider to the right. For versions **without Face ID**, press and hold the **side or top button** until the **slider** appears, then drag the **slider** to the right. With any version, you can also go to **Settings > General > Shut Down**.

- Turn on your iPhone: Hold down the **side or top button** until the Apple logo appears.

Erasing Your Apple Watch SE

There are situations you may need to erase your Apple Watch. if you forgot your passcode, for example.

Erase Apple Watch and settings

- Launch the **Settings app** on your Apple Watch.

- Go to **General > Reset,** tap **Erase All Content and Settings**, then key in your passcode.

- If your Apple Watch SE has a cellular plan, you're offered two options—**Erase All and Erase All & Keep Plan.** To completely erase your Watch, choose **Erase All.** If you want to erase and then restore it with your cellular plan in place, choose **Erase All & Keep Plan.**

- You can also open the **Apple Watch app** on your iPhone, tap **My Watch,** go to **General > Reset,** then tap **Erase Apple Watch Content and Settings.**

- If you can't access the Settings app on your Apple Watch SE because you've forgotten your passcode, put the Watch on its charger, then press and hold the **side button** until you see Power Off. Press and hold the **Digital Crown,** then tap **Reset.**

After the reset finishes and your Apple Watch restarts, you need to pair your Apple Watch with your iPhone again—open the Apple Watch app on your iPhone, then follow the instructions shown on your iPhone and Apple Watch.

Removing Your Cellular Plan

If your Apple Watch SE has cellular, you can remove the cellular plan at any time.

- Go to the **Apple Watch app** on your iPhone.

- Tap **My Watch,** tap **Cellular,** then tap (i) next to your cellular plan.

- Tap **Remove [name of carrier] Plan,** and affirm your choice.

- If need be, you have to contact your carrier to remove this Apple Watch from your cellular plan.

Forcing Your Apple Watch SE to restart

If you are unable to turn off your Apple Watch or if the problem continues, you may have to force your Apple Watch to restart. You are to do this only if you are unable to restart your Apple Watch.

- To force a restart, hold down the **side button** and the **Digital Crown** at the same time for at least ten seconds, until the Apple logo appears

Backing up and Restoring Apple Watch SE

- Back up your Apple Watch: When paired with an iPhone, Apple Watch content is constantly backed up to the iPhone. When you unpair the devices, a backup is done first.

- Restore your Apple Watch from a backup: when you pair your Apple Watch with the same iPhone again, or purchase a new Apple Watch, you can choose **Restore from Backup** and select a stored backup on your iPhone.

- An Apple Watch that's managed for a family member backs up directly to the family member's iCloud account when the watch is connected to power and a Wi-Fi network. To deactivate iCloud backups for that watch, open the **Settings app** on the managed Apple Watch, go to [account name] > **iCloud** > **iCloud Backups**, then turn off **iCloud Backups.**

Updating Apple Watch Software

It's possible for you to update your Apple Watch software by checking for updates in the **Apple Watch app** on your iPhone. You can check periodically for updates.

Checking for and Install Software Updates

- Open the **Apple Watch app** on your iPhone.

- Tap **My Watch, go to General > Software Update**, then, if an update is available, tap **Download and Install.**

If you forget Your Apple Watch Passcode

In the eventuality that your Apple Watch is disabled because you forgot your passcode or keyed in an incorrect passcode too many times, you can use the **Apple Watch app** on your iPhone to let you to key in the passcode again. If you still can't remember your passcode, you can reset Apple Watch, reset the passcode and restore Apple Watch from a backup. Restoring wipes off the content and settings on your Apple Watch, but uses a backup to replace your data and settings.

If Erase Data is turned activated, the data on your Apple Watch would be wiped after 10 failed passcode attempts.

www.ingramcontent.com/pod-product-compliance
Lightning Source LLC
LaVergne TN
LVHW051654050326
832903LV00032B/3807